Comida sana con MiPirámide/Healthy Eating with MyPyramid

# El grupo de la leche/The Milk Group

por/by Mari C. Schuh

**Traducción/Translation:** Dr. Martín Luis Guzmán Ferrer
**Editor Consultor/Consulting Editor:** Dra. Gail Saunders-Smith

**Consultor/Consultant:** Barbara J. Rolls, PhD
Guthrie Chair in Nutrition
The Pennsylvania State University
University Park, Pennsylvania

Mankato, Minnesota

Pebble Plus is published by Capstone Press,
151 Good Counsel Drive, P.O. Box 669, Mankato, Minnesota 56002.
www.capstonepress.com


Printed in the United States of America

1 2 3 4 5 6 11 10 09 08 07 06

*Library of Congress Cataloging-in-Publication Data*
Schuh, Mari C., 1975–
[Milk group. English & Spanish]
El grupo de la leche = The milk group/de/by Mari C. Schuh.
p. cm.—(Comida sana con MiPirámide = Healthy eating with MyPyramid)
Includes index.
Parallel text in English and Spanish.
ISBN-13: 978-0-7368-6669-9 (hardcover)
ISBN-10: 0-7368-6669-8 (hardcover)
1. Dairy products—Juvenile literature. 2. Nutrition—Juvenile literature. I. Title.
TX377.S3818 2007
641.3'71—dc22 2005037333

Summary: Simple text and photographs present the milk group, the foods in this group, and examples of healthy eating choices—in both English and Spanish.

**Credits**
Katy Kudela, bilingual editor; Eida del Risco, Spanish copy editor; Jennifer Bergstrom, designer; Kelly Garvin, photo researcher; Stacy Foster and Michelle Biedscheid, photo shoot coordinators

**Photo Credits**
Capstone Press/Karon Dubke, cover, 5, 6–7, 9, 11, 12–13, 15, 16–17, 19, 21, 22 (all)
Getty Images Inc./Seymour Hewitt, 1
U.S. Department of Agriculture, 8, 9 (inset)

Capstone Press thanks Hilltop Hy-Vee employees in Mankato, Minnesota, for their helpful assistance with photo shoots.

**Information in this book supports the U.S. Department of Agriculture's MyPyramid for Kids food guidance system found at http://www.MyPyramid.gov/kids. Food amounts listed in this book are based on an 1,800-calorie food plan.**

**The U.S. Department of Agriculture (USDA) does not endorse any products, services, or organizations.**

## Note to Parents and Teachers

The Comida sana con MiPirámide/Healthy Eating with MyPyramid set supports national science standards related to nutrition and physical health. This book describes the milk group in both English and Spanish. The images support early readers in understanding the text. The repetition of words and phrases helps early readers learn new words. This book also introduces early readers to subject-specific vocabulary words, which are defined in the Glossary section. Early readers may need assistance to read some words and to use the Table of Contents, Glossary, Internet Sites, and Index sections of the book.

# Table of Contents



# Tabla de contenidos

## The Milk Group

Milk, cheese, yogurt.

How many dairy products

have you had today?

## El grupo de la leche

Leche, queso, yogurt.

¿Cuántos productos lácteos

has comido hoy?

KEMPS
Select
FAT FREE
SKIM MILK
HyVee
LOWFAT
YOGURT
Strawberry Banana
WITH OTHER NATURAL FLAVORS
SINGLES
16 Singles
Swiss Style
Yoplait
Light
HyVee
MILD
CHEDDAR
HyVee
Natural
MILD
CHEDDAR
FARMS
Cheddar
40% LESS FAT
Crisper
Humidity Control

Foods in the milk group have calcium. Your bones and teeth need calcium to grow healthy and strong.

Los alimentos en el grupo de la leche tienen calcio. Tus huesos y tus dientes necesitan calcio para que crezcas sano y fuerte.

## MyPyramid for Kids

MyPyramid teaches you how much to eat from each food group. The milk group is part of MyPyramid.

## MiPirámide para niños

MiPirámide te enseña cuánto debes comer de cada uno de los grupos de alimentos. El grupo de la leche es parte de MiPirámide.

To learn more about healthy eating, go to this web site: www.MyPyramid.gov/kids Ask an adult for help.

Para saber más sobre comida sana, ve a este sitio de Internet: www.MyPyramid.gov/kids Pídele a un adulto que te ayude.

MyPyramid
For Kids
Eat Right. Exercise. Have Fun.
MyPyramid.gov
Grains
Vegetables
Fruits
Milk
Meat & Beans
USDA
DELL

Kids should eat and drink 3 cups from the milk group every day.

Los niños deben beber y comer 3 tazas del grupo de la leche todos los días.

BLUE BUNNY
Lite 85
Fat Free Skim
Grip'n
GO

## Enjoying the Milk Group

Wow! Look at all the kinds of milk. Choose low-fat milk and low-fat dairy foods.

## Cómo disfrutar de la leche

¡Guau! Mira cuántas clases de leche hay. Escoge leche baja en grasas y productos lácteos bajos en grasas.

buttermilk
buttermilk
half&half
half&half
New Era
Fat Free Skim Milk
chocolate
chocolate
two
two
Frosted Chex
New Bigger Chex Squares, Same Great Frosting
Crystal Farms
Marble Jack

White, pink, brown.

If you don´t like white milk,

try chocolate or strawberry.

Which one is your favorite?

Blanco, rosa o marrón.

Si no te gusta la leche

blanca, prueba la de

chocolate o la de fresa.

¿Cuál prefieres?

5 A DAY
for better health
SHAKE WELL
Go
SHAKE

Sweet, smooth, and creamy.
Dip fruit in your yogurt
for a tasty treat.

Dulce, suavecito y cremoso.
Mete frutas en el yogurt
y verás qué sabroso.

Nutrition Facts

Hard, soft, yellow, or white.
Find many kinds of low-fat cheese
at your grocery store.

Duro, suave, amarillo o blanco.
Busca cuántas clases de quesos
bajos en grasas hay en tu mercado.

Cracker Barrel
Velveeta
SINGLES
KRAFT
PRICE DECLINE
Deli Deluxe
72 SLICES
Berry Burst
Cheerios
HyVee

The milk group is
a part of a healthy meal.
What are your favorite foods
made from milk?

El grupo de la leche es
parte de una comida sana.
¿Cuáles son tus alimentos
preferidos hechos de leche?

# How Much to Eat/Cuánto hay que comer

Most kids need to have 3 cups from the milk group every day. To get 3 cups, pick three of your favorite milk products below.

La mayoría de los niños necesita tres tazas de alimentos lácteos al día. Para completar tres tazas, escoge tres de tus productos lácteos preferidos entre los siguientes.

**Pick three of your favorite milk products to enjoy today!**

**¡Escoge tres de tus productos lácteos preferidos!**

# Glossary

**calcium**—a mineral that the body uses to build teeth and bones

**dairy**—foods that are made with milk; milk, cheese, and yogurt are kinds of dairy foods.

**MyPyramid**—a food plan that helps kids make healthy food choices and reminds kids to be active; MyPyramid was made by the U.S. Department of Agriculture.

# Glosario

**el calcio**—mineral que el cuerpo usa para que crezcan los dientes y los huesos

**los lácteos**—alimentos que se hacen con leche; la leche, el queso y el yogurt son diferentes tipos de alimentos lácteos.

**MiPirámide**—plan de alimentos que ayuda a los chicos a escoger comidas saludables y a mantenerse activos; MiPirámide fue creada por el Departamento de Agricultura de los Estados Unidos.

# Index



# Internet Sites

FactHound offers a safe, fun way to find Internet sites related to this book. All of the sites on FactHound have been researched by our staff.

Here's how:

1. Visit *www.facthound.com*
2. Choose your grade level.
3. Type in this book ID **0736866698** for age-appropriate sites. You may also browse subjects by clicking on letters, or by clicking on pictures and words.
4. Click on the **Fetch It** button.

**FactHound will fetch the best sites for you!**

# Índice



# Sitios de Internet

FactHound proporciona una manera divertida y segura de encontrar sitios de Internet relacionados con este libro. Nuestro personal ha investigado todos los sitios de FactHound. Es posible que los sitios no estén en español.

Se hace así:

1. Visita *www.facthound.com*
2. Elige tu grado escolar.
3. Introduce este código especial **0736866698** para ver sitios apropiados según tu edad, o usa una palabra relacionada con este libro para hacer una búsqueda general.
4. Haz clic en el botón **Fetch It**.

**¡FactHound buscará los mejores sitios para ti!**